Unsettled Questions
on
Regulatory Reform

Unsettled Questions on Regulatory Reform

Paul W. MacAvoy, editor
John W. Barnum
Stephen G. Breyer
Lloyd N. Cutler
Hendrik S. Houthakker
Paul Joskow
Roger G. Noll

Merton J. Peck
Sam Peltzman
Glen O. Robinson
John E. Robson
Antonin Scalia
John W. Snow
Richard E. Wiley

American Enterprise Institute for Public Policy Research
Washington, D.C.

Library of Congress Cataloging in Publication Data
Main entry under title:
Unsettled questions on regulatory reform.

(AEI studies ; 226)
1. Independent regulatory commissions—United States—
Congresses. I. Barnum, John W., 1928–
II. MacAvoy, Paul W. III. Series: American Enterprise
Institute for Public Policy Research. AEI studies ; 226.
JK901.U6 353.09'1 78-26166
ISBN 0-8447-3328-8

AEI Studies 226

Printed in the United States of America

PARTICIPANTS

John W. Barnum
Partner, White & Case
Deputy Secretary of Transportation (1973–1977)

Stephen G. Breyer
Professor of Law, Harvard University
Attorney, Department of Justice (1965–1967)
Special Counsel, Subcommittee on Administrative Practice and Procedure,
Senate Judiciary Committee (1974–1975)

Lloyd N. Cutler
Partner, Wilmer, Cutler & Pickering

Hendrik S. Houthakker
Professor of Economics, Harvard University
Member, Council of Economic Advisers (1969–1971)

Paul Joskow
Professor of Economics, Massachusetts Institute of Technology
Co-Editor, *Bell Journal of Economics*

Paul W. MacAvoy (Moderator)
Professor of Economics and Management, Yale University
Member, Council of Economic Advisers (1975–1977)
Co-Chairman of President Ford's Domestic Council Review Group on
Regulatory Reform

Roger G. Noll
Professor of Economics, California Institute of Technology
Director, Brookings Institution Government Regulation Studies (1970–1973)
Senior Staff Economist, Council of Economic Advisers (1967–1969)

Merton J. Peck
Professor of Economics, Yale University
Member, Council of Economic Advisers (1968–1969)

Sam Peltzman
Professor of Business Economics, University of Chicago
Senior Staff Economist, Council of Economic Advisers (1970–1971)
Co-Editor, *Journal of Political Economy*

Glen O. Robinson
Professor of Law, University of Virginia
Commissioner, Federal Communications Commission (1974–1976)

John E. Robson
Executive Vice President, G. D. Searle & Company
Undersecretary of Transportation (1968–1969)
Chairman, Civil Aeronautics Board (1975–1977)

Antonin Scalia
Professor of Law, University of Chicago
Chairman, Administrative Conference of the United States (1972–1974)
Assistant Attorney General, Office of Legal Counsel (1974–1976)

John W. Snow
Vice President, The Chessie System
Deputy Undersecretary, Department of Transportation (1975–1976)
Administrator, National Highway Traffic Safety Administration (1976–1977)

Richard E. Wiley
Partner, Kirkland & Ellis
Chairman, Federal Communications Commission (1974–1977)

This panel discussion was part of a conference on
Regulation and Regulatory Reform,
sponsored by the Center for the Study of Government Regulation
of the American Enterprise Institute
and held at the Washington Hilton Hotel, Washington, D.C.,
on December 19, 1977.

PREFACE

The regulatory agencies, boards, and commissions comprise a large and growing "fourth branch" of our national government. They answer only to a limited extent to the executive, legislative, or judiciary branches, and they form such an amorphous group that someone recently suggested that they comprise the "fourth to twentieth" branches of government in Washington. Yet there are some aspects of what the commissions do which are the same. These aspects make up a "process" and produce "results" that in the last five years have caused strong reactions among policy makers.

Some of the reactions have been positive. The process, while costly, has shown elements of "fairness" and of concern for those with little political or economic power. The results seem to have been sufficiently in line with the goals of legislation to convince Congress that regulation was worth trying when it came time to deal with energy prices and auto emissions in the last five years.

But most recently the reactions have been more negative than positive. The process has been seen as unduly burdensome and costly, and the results either too much in favor of particular interests or too blunt to meet the needs of consumers, workers, or whomever. These have given rise to a reform movement, directed mostly towards reducing controls through new legislation and through changing the policy makers within the commissions. As the movement has grown, however, the amount of actual deregulation has not increased significantly. Indeed, by most measures the total amount of regulation has increased. There have been problems of "process" and "results" in reform, just as there have been in regulation.

These problems are addressed here by a group of professors, lawyers, and commission members long experienced in both regulation and its reform. The questions that must be answered to make reform more effective are:

- Why has so little reform been accomplished?
- Has the case for deregulation been made?
- What are the priority areas for reform?
- Where is regulation having the greatest effect?
- What changes should be made in the reform process?

Although they could have been asked in another order, this sequence produced some important if preliminary answers that should make it possible to change these government activities more rapidly and for the better. The answers are not grandiose or inspiring; rather they center on critical detail, on hard political choices of program content, and on the content of leadership in the White House and Congress. But these matters determine whether anything gets done.

PAUL W. MACAVOY
Yale School of Organization and Management
New Haven, Connecticut

1
Why Has So Little Reform Been Accomplished?

PROFESSOR MACAVOY: Attempts to reform regulation are as old as regulation itself. The pace of reform efforts has quickened in the last decade, however, with both more legislation to deregulate and more frequent attempts at internal improvements in process within the agencies. But given these frequent and highly publicized attempts, why has so little actual reform taken place in the last decade?

PROFESSOR SCALIA: Deregulation is not just a matter of altering government activity; rather, it represents a fundamental shift in social philosophy from government interventionism, which has increasingly characterized our society since the days of the New Deal, toward belief in the free market—toward willingness to rely on the free market to benefit society. Now, that takes some doing. The way government goes depends not so much upon the realities as upon the public perception of the realities at the time. And that perception, for many years, has been that "there oughta to be a law"—that most areas will profit from government control. Changing that public perception takes a long time; indeed, I would be fearful if it could be done quickly because that would speak rather poorly for the stability of our society.

PROFESSOR PELTZMAN: Something has been accomplished, but obviously reform has not gone very far. Why? In a broad sense, reform has not gone very far because the time has not been right. It has not been right in the sense that many regulatory agencies not only impose what we economists like to call "deadweight losses" or inefficiencies on the industries they regulate, but they also transfer a large amount of income. It is never easy to make a fundamental change when a result of that change will be large shifts of income.

But we do tend to get progress when the time is right. The biggest current push toward deregulation seems to be in the airline industry. We can date the beginning of this movement to the 1970 investigation of domestic passenger fares by the Civil Aeronautics Board (CAB). What emerged from that investigation was the realization that in fact the industry had large inefficiencies in relation to the amount of income that was being transferred. Thus, the CAB itself began to feel the pressure to make regulation more rational and took some steps in that direction. The momentum began to gather, and it is still gathering. Basically, progress will occur because, whatever the shouting is about, the inefficiencies in the industry are large relative to the amount of income that is being shifted around. And when we get to that state in other industries, a similar momentum will develop.

DR. SNOW: The asymmetry of the congressional process also plays an important role here. The burden of proof on those seeking to change regulation is enormous. They must have studies that show who will provide what service where, when, and at what prices after reform. They must demonstrate that chaos will not occur, that people in rural communities will continue to receive service. This is the case even though the proponents of regulation never had to meet any similar burden of proof when the regulations were first set in place. The point is that one of the reasons that reform is slow is this asymmetry with respect to regulating "quickly" and then deregulating "eventually."

PROFESSOR JOSKOW: The answer depends very much on what we mean by regulatory reform—do we mean deregulation, or less regulation, or changes in the way we go about regulation? In the category of deregulation, our successes have been rather limited. We have been talking about airline deregulation for quite a long time, but our success in actually getting a bill passed through the Congress came only after a determined set of new commissioners and CAB staff started to do the job unilaterally. They were able to show that the benefits of competition could be achieved without the predicted dire consequences for the airlines.

In the area of surface transportation, not much progress has been made, and it does not look like very much progress will be made unless a concerted effort to build on the airline example is made. I believe that the reason for the lack of progress is the large income transfers that have resulted from the current regulatory regime and the kinds of new transfers that would result from a transition from a regulated regime to an unregulated one.

In the area of regulation of financial institutions, especially regulation of the insurance industry, there has been some success. Since 1968 there has been a gradual reform on the state level, a movement away from heavy reliance on rate regulation toward greater reliance on the market. I must report, however, that in my own state of Massachusetts deregulation lasted approximately six months. In this instance, not surprisingly, the advent of deregulation produced many predictable results, including changes in driver classification schemes, rate levels, and the rate structure. Unfortunately, those changes resulted in dramatic increases in the price of automobile insurance for certain groups of people—specifically, poor people, black people, city people. This attracted tremendous newspaper coverage and stimulated political controversy, which led the newborn effort at deregulation to abort. I will be surprised if that deregulation effort occurs again in the future.

To improve on those results, we economists have a twofold task. In the long run, we must deal with the kinds of income redistribution that are going to be associated with deregulation. In the short run, we must try to deal with the problems that are going to arise during the transition to deregulation. In sum, the role of economists is to present the information required to understand the deregulation process, and to chart more fully a transition course that will perhaps be more politically feasible than some of the proposals we have made in the past.

PROFESSOR MACAVOY: As staff director of the Administrative Practices Subcommittee of the Senate Judiciary Committee, Stephen Breyer initiated an effort to assess and evaluate regulation of the airlines. This effort produced the early drafts of the bill by Senator Edward Kennedy (Democrat, Massachusetts) to reduce airline regulation. When Professor Breyer left Massachusetts for Washington, he said he would have regulatory reform won and the troops home before Christmas. Three years later much the same bill passed and was signed into law, and the question is why was this reform such a long-term and highly detailed process?

PROFESSOR BREYER: I think that the work of the subcommittee illustrates that the process of regulatory reform can be reasonably successful. One reason for the success of that effort is that it was a joint effort by people in the Ford administration such as John Barnum and John Snow together with liberal Democrats on Capitol Hill. It was understood that airline regulatory reform did not belong to one party or another. And the effort produced results. One result was that John Robson was appointed chairman of the Civil Aeronautics Board and began the movement to deregulate at the board. Another result was the appointment of Alfred Kahn as John Robson's successor at CAB. Moreover, I do not think that any other agency in government has among its top staff members so many people who believe so strongly in the competitive process.

Now, is it enough that a regulatory agency is run by people who believe in the competitive process? There is no simple answer. But many changes have in fact occurred over the last three years in the marketplace: discount fares have been reintroduced, minimum charter rates have been abolished, the route moratorium has been destroyed, and Freddy Laker's airline has entered the international market. Other airlines are responding to Laker's low fares and prices are going down. The competitive process is working. Thus, considerable change has occurred in the airline industry. And, looking at both the present makeup of the CAB and the new law, there is reason to believe that change will continue.

PROFESSOR MACAVOY: Professor Breyer, would you comment on John Snow's assertion that the process is prolonged and made less efficient because those proposing deregulation must bear the burden of proof?

PROFESSOR BREYER: The people who want change usually have the burden of proof. If regulation currently exists, then the people who want to bring about change had better show that something is seriously wrong with the present system and that there is a good alternative. They have to make a strong enough case so that the Congress has to pay attention to them.

PROFESSOR MACAVOY: The point of my question was not whether the deregulators should prove that reform is needed, but whether those seeking to deregulate are being required to bear a greater burden of proof than were those seeking to impose regulation in the first place. I would submit that, if we examine the legislative history underlying the Civil Aeronautics Act of 1938, we will not find studies demonstrating chaos in the aviation industry in the period from 1935 to 1938, nor any proof that the bill would be the means to improve on actual market conditions of the time.

PROFESSOR BREYER: No, but there was another argument for regulation during that particular era—corruption had been uncovered in the previous system. A problem existed; there was a demand for some solution; and regulation was seen as that solution.

PROFESSOR MACAVOY: But the problem was not chaos in the industry, and yet the current justification for not changing the statute has been that chaos would return to airline markets.

PROFESSOR BREYER: It is interesting to recall the legislative history of that 1939 act. Colonel Dorell, who was the Air Transport Association's primary witness, was asked if there had in fact been destructive competition in the airline industry, and he replied, no, but he worried about what might happen. The second person who testified was Amelia Earhart, and she said she did not like the bill very much, because the CAB might never let anybody in the industry. Then, Senator Harry Truman, who was running the hearing, said, "My God, you have to trust somebody, don't you?"

PROFESSOR MACAVOY: Has the pace of change in communications industry regulation and in surface transportation regulation been more rapid?

MR. WILEY: Five years ago, when I became chairman of the Federal Communications Commission, we began a modest program to reduce the regulation of small radio stations. At that time, we considered the term "deregulation" too controversial, and so we coined the phrase "reregulation." At that time, the view on Capitol Hill toward regulatory reform was neutral at best and possibly hostile. Much of this opposition has now changed. Of course, certain vested interests are still greatly opposed to reform. Serious thinkers in this area, however, are virtually unanimous in the view that there ought to be more reliance on the marketplace and less on regulation. Thus, some progress has been made.

What has to be done in the future is to transfer this viewpoint to the general public. I am not certain that the broad range of the American public has been totally sold on the virtues of deregulation. As I discovered when I was at the FCC, many people still believe that it is up to the government to protect their private interests.

PROFESSOR PECK: The early history of the Interstate Commerce Commission (ICC) provides us with an interesting example. Although the ICC was established in 1887, it took until about 1906 for the commission to produce really effective regulations for the railroad industry. Over that twenty-year period, the commission built up "social capital"— that is, an atmosphere of public approval that other regulated industries could profit from later. I think we may be going through another historical watershed. If airline deregulation is achieved and is successful, "social capital" may be built up that will facilitate deregulation in other sectors. What the historical example really demonstrates is that change is difficult in either direction.

PROFESSOR MACAVOY: Is there a dissenting view on this question?

PROFESSOR HOUTHAKKER: My view is that the effort to reform regulation has actually moved backward, not forward. This can be demonstrated by going beyond the traditional areas of regulation on which most of the discussion has centered so far. Some progress has been made in certain areas of transportation, in securities regulation, and perhaps in communications. On the other hand, large new fields that previously were more or less unregulated, or only partially regulated, have become very fully regulated. I am thinking particularly of the energy area outside of the traditional electric power and gas fields. In those cases, there has been a proliferation of regulatory efforts, and there is no end in sight. A new regulatory agency—the Commodity Futures Trading Commission, which partly replaces an older agency—has been established. That is another addition to regulation. I am not saying now whether it is a good or bad addition; I think this particular agency has the potential of being useful. The steel industry becomes regulated as the "reference price system" is actually adopted. This is simply a new and unusual form of regulation. Thus, the question is not why has so little been accomplished, but why are we still sliding back?

2

Has the Case for Deregulation Been Made?

PROFESSOR MACAVOY: A substantial amount of economic research underlies the position on regulation that most economists seem to share at the present time. That position is that regulation is not now working well to achieve its economic and social objectives, and that it should be cut back. But is this research adequate? Is the economists' position sufficiently well grounded? Has the case for deregulation been made effectively in economic and political analysis?

MR. BARNUM: This question triggers two observations on my part. The first is illustrated by what happened in the case of surface transportation reregulation or deregulation. The various attempts to achieve regulatory reform in surface transportation did not get very far until the Penn Central and other railroads went bankrupt a few years ago. Even then, the Railroad Revitalization and Regulatory Reform Act that the Congress passed in December 1975 included a great deal of money for the railroads generally and for the Northeast Corridor in particular, but not much administrative reform of the ICC. It was only because the President stood firm and said he would not sign the bill that the congressional committees rewrote the bill to include some regulatory reform. In short, the President agreed to put several billion dollars into the bankrupt railroads and several billion dollars more into the Northeast Corridor on the condition that the Congress give him substantial regulatory reform. Thus, the regulatory reform that we achieved in the railroad industry was not the result of extensive economic analysis and presentation; it was very simply the result of political leverage. This reform, moreover, was very much watered down and subsequently aborted in some respects by the Interstate Commerce Commission.

My second observation is that I question whether the case that has been made for deregulation by some economists, and certainly by some politicians, is one that we can consider satisfactory. Much of the attractiveness of aviation regulatory reform to the general public—and, hence, the reason for some of the steam behind it in the Congress—is the belief, fed by many economists and politicians, that deregulation will cause airline fares to go down 40 percent across the board. This is not going to happen, and if all fares do not go down 40 percent, any subsequent regulatory reform effort for other phases of transportation is going to face serious credibility problems. Thus I question whether the economic case for deregulation based on promised immediate consumer gains has been made successfully.

PROFESSOR BREYER: If we compare the price of a cross-country airline ticket on a discount fare today with the price in December 1975, we discover that the difference is roughly 40 percent. And if we compare the price of a transatlantic ticket on Freddy Laker's airline or on one of the minimum rate charter flights with the price of a regular ticket on one of the major airlines, we see a dramatic reduction. Although I agree with John Barnum's general point, I think that, in the case of airlines, fares can go down a lot and they have.

PROFESSOR MACAVOY: To make the argument that the research on deregulation was adequate, however, we would have to declare that deregulation caused these fare reductions in the Civil Aeronautics Board before the bill was passed.

PROFESSOR BREYER: A point that Professor Peltzman made earlier is worth stressing here. One of the reasons that people went after the CAB in 1975 was that the board choked off all price competition. They had limited entry into the market so severely that it was possible to get both economists and industry to agree that some change was needed. In that context, regulatory reform meant introducing more competition. Since 1975, even without a bill, more competition was gradually introduced because of the presence of reformers on the board. In a sense, that is reform because a more liberal rate policy was adopted and because more firms will be allowed into the industry. Of course, the institution now has been changed so that, when these individual board members leave, the same policies will be continued.

PROFESSOR ROBINSON: From what I have seen in communications, the economists' case for regulatory change has been made, but it has not been believed. In a sense, the economists have not made their case to the people who are controlling the policy—they have not made it to the public, the broadcasters, the telephone industry, or the FCC. What has gone wrong? Part of the problem is the income transfer question that was discussed earlier. People do not want to hear about misallocation of resources; they just want to hear about who wins and who loses, and those who would lose under deregulation are in the driver's seat right now. Thus, the question is not whether the case has been made, but whether the case will be believed even if it has been made.

Independent of communications, however, the case for deregulation has in general been made largely to the "already-committed." We have been preaching to believers who readily assent to the case. But, according to recent samplings of public opinion, the majority of Americans want more, not less, regulation. Why? One possible explanation is that the economists have not learned how to talk to the public.

PROFESSOR NOLL: Economists have not proven the case for deregulation, but they cannot do so because that is not within their disciplinary capabilities. Given this, economists have done about as good a job as can be expected of them in most areas. For example, economists agree that any attempt to improve the efficiency of transportation by regulating competition is doomed to failure—from the standpoint of efficiency, such an attempt is bound to impose substantial net costs. Nevertheless, there are some issues about which we cannot speak with the same authority. The first issue is one that Professor Joskow raised—namely, the dynamic aspects of the "transition problem." Virtually all of the economic research comparing deregulated with regulated transportation demonstrates that the deregulated state is more efficient than the other, but price, output, and income distribution during the process of deregulation have not been assessed. In fact, economists have a range of inconsistent points of view on such transition conditions, based in part on different views about the expectations of those involved in buying and selling during such dislocations. But regulatory reform should not have to wait until economists assess transition problems because, in fact, they do not now have sufficient empirical evidence about the transition to a deregulated state in an industry to demonstrate their theories.

A second important point is that economists cannot come up with hard and fast estimates of the costs of present regulation. We have statistical and mathematical techniques for modeling that enable us to make quantitative statements, but the fact remains that today estimates of the economic inefficiencies caused by surface transportation regulation range from a few hundred million dollars to $20 billion. I recently attended a conference at which a heated debate took place about whether the cost of federal regulation of oil was $2 billion a year or $15 billion a year. Even given the amount of money at issue, economists cannot resolve these disputes. But the fact is that members of Congress and politicians in general respond to such a range of estimates by believing that economists have nothing to say. They listen to the debate about matters such as whose econometric model is better without recognizing that we all think the inefficiency in that kind of regulation is significant.

A third point is that economists know almost nothing about the effects of noneconomic regulation, such as regulation of health, safety, or the environment, because our modeling techniques and methods of analysis are based largely on market results. We know very little about how to model qualitative effects, and we have great difficulty inferring things about values that are not transacted in markets. At the same time, the theoretical case for imposing such regulation, except for environmental problems and highly complex, long-term health effects, is quite weak.

Finally, economists have turned almost no attention to assessing the regulated monopolies. We have spent very little time analyzing ways to improve such industries with institutional change. Again, it is difficult to prove anything in that category because of the absence of empirical observations on alternatives to existing arrangements.

What I see, then, is a limited role for economists. We can do comparative institutional analyses, and we have something to say about economic efficiencies. We have very little to say, however, about what processes are more fair than others, or about what members of society can be best protected by what institutions. But this is my point: economists have done about all that they can be expected to do.

PROFESSOR SCALIA: After telling us all of the things that economists can do, Professor Noll, why do you say that economists cannot tell us anything about the transitional effects?

PROFESSOR NOLL: I am not saying that. What I am saying is that, as a matter of fact, we do not have the modeling and statistical equipment with which to answer questions about the path between one equilibrium and another. We have little to say about the transitional effects because the science of economics has not yet been developed to the point at which questions involving dynamics can be analyzed with the same degree of sophistication as questions involving static comparisons.

PROFESSOR SCALIA: My initial response to the question of whether or not the case for deregulation has been made is to ask, To whom do you expect to make the case? Ultimately, it has to be made to the public, and I think that is beginning to happen. Of course, convincing the public takes a long time and thus change will be slow. On balance, I think that is probably a good thing.

Without denigrating the work of economists, it is conceivable that some of their calls for deregulation are as erroneous as many of their earlier calls for regulation. I am quite content to see the change come gradually, as the economists' work percolates down and ultimately (to the extent it is valid) produces some solid national consensus. I think that is in the process of occurring.

PROFESSOR MACAVOY: At some stage in their work on airline deregulation, John Snow and Stephen Breyer were both faced with assertions that chaos and disruption would result in the industry. They went to work to determine whether that was likely. What were the results?

DR. SNOW: The principal argument made against the air bill was that service to small communities would collapse with deregulation. Proponents of the status quo argued that regulation assured service to small communities, that regulation assured an individual that he could go from a small town in South Dakota to O'Hare Airport in Chicago and then down to Miami. Analyses in the Department of Transportation indicated that, even in a totally deregulated environment, most communities were likely to continue having good air service. With respect to the service quality issue, economic analysis showed that chaos would not result and that, indeed, small towns would continue to get air service.

There were potential transition problems, and work had to be done to predict magnitudes. We were concerned that regulation had created excess capacity and that if the floodgates of competition were opened too rapidly, the excess capacity would press on the market and drive rates down more than 40 percent, and possibly as much as 60 percent for some period of time. Since that could precipitate bankruptcies and attendant serious political problems, such possibilities had to be investigated, and this was done on a case-by-case basis, using market and investment analysis. This work made the case that chaos would not result. Those were the elements of the intellectual backing for the air bill.

PROFESSOR BREYER: The example of airline deregulation illustrates how the reform effort demands cooperation among people in different institutions and different disciplines. An economist like James C. Miller III presents five good arguments about why it is unlikely that there will be a problem with service to small communities. A lawyer then organizes those arguments into the proper adversarial structure for a congressional hearing. The economists provide the conceptual framework, and the lawyers get people to produce evidence, because the economists do not have all the evidence.

This evidence is of two kinds. First are the studies done for and within the Department of Transportation on industry supply, demand, and financing. Second is the evidence provided by the airlines themselves. We would go to United Airlines, for example, and say, "Let's analyze your routes one by one." Sitting there and going over the system route by route, we would end up agreeing that there are only, say, 27 routes out of 350 on which the firm's incremental revenues are exceeded by their incremental costs. We would ask them how much of their revenue passenger miles those routes accounted for, and they would reply that it was a very small percentage. Even though such research is impressionistic, it has political value. It assures members of Congress and the general public that the researcher has actually been out there in the industry, and it gives added political weight to the congressman who is reluctant to depend solely on those thick research studies prepared for the Department of Transportation.

PROFESSOR JOSKOW: One would think, from this discussion, that the rank-and-file of economists are marching shoulder to shoulder upon Washington with similar opinions. In the case of the airlines, that impression would be fairly accurate. For a variety of reasons, economists have been in general agreement about the wisdom of regulatory reform in the airline industry. As we move from airlines to trucks, there is probably still quite a bit of agreement. When we go to energy, however, some of those ranks start to break off, and, if we go to telecommunications, we have two or three separate armies hurling indirect utility functions and production functions at one another. If we go to environmental, occupational safety, and health regulation, there is probably no agreement at all about what controls are good or bad.

PROFESSOR HOUTHAKKER: I do not think the case for regulatory reform has been made, but this is not because of the defects in empirical studies. What we have not yet done is to give the public a conceptual framework on the whole subject of regulation. What purposes can regulation serve, and how can it best serve those purposes? What activities are outside the proper sphere of regulation? These questions have not been answered, and, as a result, the movement toward deregulation is conceptually on rather thin ice.

We have concentrated on the minuses of regulation, of which there are many; consequently, we have been accused, with some justice, of being one-sided, and we have been left out of decisions concerning new areas of regulation. I find it deplorable that in the area of energy the United States is regulating now in ways that are much worse than anything that happened in transportation or in communications, much worse than anything that the previous Federal Power Commission ever did on its own.

PROFESSOR PECK: There is a saying that economists make bullets that lawyers fire at one another. In the early 1960s, I did research in the field of transportation, and at that time no lawyers were taking the bullets. What really dictates their demands for information are matters outside the purview of economists and their profession. Once the lawyers and the politicians have started the war, then each side's supply of ammunition becomes very important, even though the ammunition supply is not the precipitating event. Thus, in my view, changes in economic knowledge are less important in precipitating regulatory reform than events outside of economics.

MR. WILEY: I do not think the bullets are hitting in the right place. Sophisticated economic arguments can convince a select audience about the virtues, values, and merits of deregulation. But we have to find ways to translate these arguments into identifiable, understandable, relatively simple measurements of public benefit from reform. The media may use rhetoric to describe the government bureaucracy strangling American free enterprise, but, beyond that, most people are not protesting against regulation so much as they are asking for the government's protection against violent programming, against an alleged deterioration of telephone service, against other perceived abuses and shortcomings in our market economy. We have to find ways to sell more directly and more simply the benefits of relying on the marketplace and on competition. Until the lawyers, economists, and politicians do that, getting reform legislation through the Congress will continue to be a problem because, after all, the Congress relies greatly upon the views of the people.

3
What Are the Priority Areas for Reform?

PROFESSOR MACAVOY: What are the priority areas for reform for the next ten years? How much of this reform can be done by the Congress, by the executive office, or by the agencies themselves?

PROFESSOR HOUTHAKKER: It is very important that the United States not go any further in opening new areas of regulation. I was quite interested in the remarks made earlier about the history of the Civil Aeronautics Act because it was clear that there was little preparation for airline regulation. I would say that the preparation for energy regulation in the last few years has not been any more substantial. As a result, we may be fighting much worse battles in years to come in the process of unwinding ill-conceived new regulations. Thus, my first priority is that, when new regulatory programs are adopted, some of the standards that are now applied in deregulation cases be applied to new regulations.

Beyond that, a comprehensive approach to regulatory reform is needed. A few years ago, I drew up a list of about forty-five different areas of overextended controls. We will not get very far by picking off these areas of regulation one by one, because then we run into the problem of congressional resistance. The congressional committee system exists, in part, to perpetuate these regulations. An omnibus bill covering a large number of areas would be treated differently from the legislation dealing only with transportation or communications. The Congress would have to appoint a special committee to treat it, bypassing the existing committees, which are on the whole a great barrier to reform. The precedent for such action has been set now because this is precisely what has been done in the case of the energy legislation.

That is my general view, but I would add that attention has to be given first to energy regulation and next to environmental regulation, about which the public has become polarized to a large extent. When I was a member of the Council of Economic Advisers, we wrote the first governmental statement on protection of the environment, in which we advocated greater use of taxes for environmental protection. This has not been done, and, as a result, the country finds itself deeper and deeper in a quagmire of regulations that are more or less contradictory. What is perhaps the most serious aspect of the control process is that some members of the environmental movement believe that, if the regulations do not stop certain types of production, they have not done their job. That approach, which sees almost any form of production as environmentally objectionable, refuses to compromise and, essentially, seeks to obstruct. This is the regulatory process gone wild, and it is on these areas that we have to concentrate our reform efforts to make progress in the near future.

PROFESSOR MACAVOY: John Snow, should safety regulation be put high on Professor Houthakker's list of overextended controls to be given priority in reform?

DR. SNOW: I spent some time as the head of the National Highway Traffic Safety Administration (NHTSA), which is responsible for regulating the motor vehicle manufacturers to advance the cause of highway safety. And I think the answer to your question has to be yes.

Agencies like NHTSA are created largely in an open-ended way. The Congress says that there is a problem of deaths and injuries on the nation's highways. They create an agency to solve the problem, but they do not tell the administrator or the staff of the agency what the time-frame is or how much of the problem the Congress thinks can be resolved through regulation. The administrator of such an agency finds himself with a strong mandate, a mandate to achieve safety with little or no consideration for the cost. Thus, there is a built-in bias to issue more and more regulation.

The Congress needs to provide better legislation to begin with; it needs to identify in the legislation the scope and magnitude of the problem that regulation is expected to solve, and thereby to specify the limitations of the regulation. It needs to consider other tools besides regulation, and it should indicate a time period for phasing out the regulation.

Because the Congress has not done this, the National Highway Traffic Safety Administration today finds itself in a situation in which new regulations are producing diminishing returns. That makes the position of the administrator of the agency most uncomfortable, because he or she is continually urged to issue more regulations. During my time in office, the agency was criticized for slowing down the pace at which regulations were issued, and we were called before congressional committees and asked to explain why we were not advancing the cause of highway safety by issuing more regulations.

PROFESSOR MACAVOY: Professor Breyer, from an administrative lawyer's view, where in the spectrum of regulation—from price controls to environmental controls—is the most inefficient and disruptive mismatch between process and results?

PROFESSOR BREYER: The question correctly implies that regulation is not a single process, but rather a number of different tools designed to deal with a number of different problems. The tools include taxes, collective bargaining techniques, and modes of governmental intervention such as price controls, entry controls, and equipment and production specifications. The goals include consumer protection against monopoly, fraud, unsafe products, and externalities. Looking at regulation from the point of view of matching tools and goals, I can suggest candidates for reform as various "mismatches." And I say "candidates" deliberately because, as is revealed in airline regulatory reform, it is a vast step from identifying a candidate for change to learning enough about the industry and the world in which it operates to know if change really should take place.

My first candidate is natural gas and crude oil price controls. To achieve the goal of transferring windfall profits from producers to consumers, one ought to consider using taxes rather than a classical cost-of-service rate-making system. The second is environmental protection—this type of regulation deals basically with adverse spillover effects from production, and some form of a price or a tax system should be considered as working better than direct output controls. The third candidate is occupational safety, which normally regulates by setting physical design standards for the workplace. Some alternatives might, however, be considered: for example, greater provision of information, some form of taxes, or forms of collective bargaining. My final candidate is the trucking industry. In the case of the trucking industry, some have argued for using antitrust action and relying upon a marketplace policed with antitrust mechanisms if there is a problem that calls for government intervention.

So, my candidates for reform are spread across regulation. I would add that reform does not mean deregulation across the board; rather, it might mean using methods—such as antitrust, taxes, and collective bargaining—that rely more upon incentives to deal with the problem that called for regulation in the first place.

PROFESSOR PELTZMAN: The areas such as energy, the environment, safety, and health, in which regulation probably has the greatest current economic impact, are also the areas that have been regulated most recently. There is a reason for that. Strong political forces are pushing for regulation in these areas, and there is little reason to expect that these forces are going to be turned aside.

I do not disagree with Professor Houthakker about the desirability of a comprehensive approach, but we need to be talking about what is likely to work. A comprehensive approach is not going to work unless there is some general political revulsion with the size of government. The forces pushing for regulation in the energy field are different from those pushing in the airline industry. The underlying tug-of-war over who gets what is probably the same, but the forces are different. Energy regulation came into being now and not in the 1930s because the Organization of Petroleum Exporting Countries (OPEC) only recently decided to triple the price of oil. This motivated a congressional response that could not await an in-depth study of the issues. In the same way as with airlines, reform here will be achieved when the time is right, and trying to include oil and gas price controls in a comprehensive deregulation bill would not be successful at this time.

For an example of when the time is right, consider drug regulation. A few years ago, somebody asked me, "What is going to happen with drug regulation?" I was brave and ventured the guess that it would become less stringent in the late 1970s. Why? In the late 1950s, the drug industry developed a large number of new drugs, and in the late 1970s I knew their patents would run out. That situation is going to change the structure of the political forces that are operating on the Food and Drug Administration. The point is that one should not expect an institutional gimmick—whether it be a bill or a stratagem to get some regulation out from under one agency and shift it to another—to have very large effects. Such gimmicks can have effects, but the effects will not be very large unless the time is right.

PROFESSOR ROBINSON: In seeking immediate targets for reform, we should not be asking what are the most egregious cases of regulation but rather what are the easiest targets for reform. We have talked about success in reforming airline regulation. There is a very good reason for going after airline reform because that is the easiest target on the landscape today. If we could not get the airlines deregulated to some important degree, we certainly could not get the trucks deregulated.

The next easiest target among the historically regulated industries is communications. The time is right. The courts have demanded some relaxation of regulations in the field of cable television, and the Federal

Communications Commission has moved to introduce some competition into telecommunications. In the telephone industry, new technologies are forcing competitive entry by firms that have not been in the communications business. These conditions all contribute to an atmosphere for reform.

We must shoot at the easy targets as they come up politically. That does not mean that we have to stand still with respect to other areas. What it does mean, however, is that, contrary to the approach advocated by President Ford and Professor Houthakker, we should not try for some kind of global strategy. That approach would simply abstract the problem to such a degree that no particular groups would be pushing for reform.

DR. SNOW: I disagree with Professor Robinson. Professor Houthakker's point—that we have lost ground and that we are continuing to lose ground—is critical. Unless we take a comprehensive approach and try to make the Congress aware of the implications of the continuing growth of governmental programs and agencies, we are fighting a losing cause. Something should be done to slow down the growth of new governmental programs at the same time that unnecessary existing programs are removed. Focusing simply on the deregulation of existing programs misses an important part of the regulatory picture.

MR. ROBSON: That is a key point. I think that, if we have a comprehensive strategy, it ought to be directed at retarding the growth of regulation. After all, reform suggests that something wrong has already been done; perhaps our efforts are better directed at preventing the wrong program from occurring in the first place. But, in terms of rolling back regulatory schemes that are already in place, a rifle shot approach is the only practical way of succeeding.

PROFESSOR SCALIA: The Ford administration tried the comprehensive approach; indeed, it introduced a bill that would have required the Congress to reexamine systematically over a period of five or seven years all areas of governmental regulation. The bill was met with resounding silence, and that is likely to be the fate of any such enterprise. Moreover, I am not very hopeful that such a bill, if it were passed, would really produce any more than a "sunset bill" would. Such actions are largely theatrical and are not likely to produce good hard thinking about all of these areas, which is what is needed. Therefore, I think it is necessary to go after reform industry by industry. To some extent, all of the sound and fury about massive deregulation diverts energies from methodical progress.

PROFESSOR BREYER: I would like to address one question to the advocates of the comprehensive approach. What should we do about those instances in which regulation is right? I think there are cases—and communications might be one—in which regulation is desirable. How does this condition fit into the comprehensive approach?

PROFESSOR HOUTHAKKER: The comprehensive approach certainly does not mean that we would repeal all the many regulatory laws that are now on the statute books. Choices have to be made. Moreover, the comprehensive approach does not mean that we would use a shotgun technique in which we fire indiscriminately at every target in sight. The targets have to be carefully selected.

With the comprehensive approach, moreover, we can form new coalitions to push for reform. Take the truckers, for instance. Over the years, they have been very clever at preventing any meaningful reform in trucking regulation—with one or two exceptions, such as the agricultural exemption. But the truckers have interests other than trucking regulations. For example, energy regulation could possibly become a serious problem for the trucking industry at some point. At that point, the potential exists for a kind of support—for energy and trucking reform together—that is not present in a piece-by-piece approach.

Currently, when reform proposals are advanced one by one, the vested interests look at a particular proposal and say, "We do not like it," and that is the end of the proposal. The history of transportation regulation offers many examples of aborted efforts at reform. Airline regulation may be changed for the better now because some airlines have changed their minds about reform. We should not, however, overlook the fact that the legislative system is biased in favor of preserving existing regulations and, indeed, of intensifying them. That is why we have to think in terms of new coalitions.

PROFESSOR MACAVOY: Are there priorities in reforming regulation of transportation?

MR. BARNUM: I think there are, and for me the priority area continues to be the rail industry. Even though a railroad regulatory reform bill was signed into law in February 1976, it has been vitiated by two reactions. First, there was the reaction to limiting rate flexibility for the railroads to areas where they do not have "market dominance." The ICC has defined market dominance in a way that effectively frustrates any rate flexibility that the railroads thought they had obtained in the legislation. Second, the Congress has stalled the effort to eliminate, or abandon, unproductive parts of the rail system.

In the negotiations between the Congress and the Ford administration over the legislation, some regulatory reform was exchanged for some financing of the railroads across the country. As part of the trade-off, the executive branch was given considerable authority to set the rate of interest for the federal financial assistance and to establish the other terms and conditions upon which it would be made available to the railroads. The intention was to induce the railroad industry to rationalize its plant, which is underutilized. But the Congress then withdrew that authority to determine the cost of financial assistance for the less effective railroads. As a result, funds are now being distributed to parts of the railroad system that should not be retained. Thus, we have slipped back and are losing ground on the railroad front, even though a reform law has been passed. Consequently, I would still give priority to railroad reform.

PROFESSOR MACAVOY: Are there priorities in reforming regulation of communications?

MR. WILEY: My answer to that question is similar to John Barnum's answer about transportation. I am concerned that we might slip backward in the area of telecommunications regulation. The FCC has made some important strides forward; it has opened up to competition areas that traditionally were dominated by monopolies. When that began to happen, a rather strong effort was mounted on Capitol Hill to reverse the situation. Approximately 200 members of Congress supported a bill that would have totally eliminated every vestige of the commission's procompetitive policies in telecommunications, which have been sustained in the court. At this point, my number one priority is to make sure that we do not lose the competition we have already won by passing that bill in forthcoming sessions.

4

Where Is Regulation Having the Greatest Effect?

PROFESSOR MACAVOY: I detect some strain between the economists and the lawyers over the term *priority areas.* The lawyers are arguing that we should seek targets of opportunity, that is, areas in which a reform program could have some impact. The economists, on the other hand, are saying that some industries are now experiencing highly adverse economic effects because of regulation and these should be the priority areas regardless of perceived political opportunities. To the extent the second view is germane, we should know where the disasters perpetrated by regulation are. I am going to ask three economists where regulation is having the most adverse effect on the economy at this time, and whether this effect has been highly adverse and thus encourages deregulation.

PROFESSOR JOSKOW: Regulation promises to have—if it does not already have—a highly adverse effect in the environmental area. The effect is adverse both in terms of economic efficiency and in terms of people's perceptions of the fairness with which the process works. In the energy area, the Carter administration's current bill has profound implications for the cost of energy and the distribution of energy resources in this country. The implications may not be felt so much tomorrow, but they probably will be felt in ten years.

In dealing with priority areas, however, one cannot attack them piece by piece. According to the "target of opportunity" argument, targets arise primarily when regulation is doing so badly that a consensus forms to change it. Railroad regulation becomes a target once the railroads really start to fall apart and somebody wants to do something about them; airline regulation becomes a target when the fares go up and up and up. The advantage of the comprehensive approach is that it can create a memory bank of experiences in the reform effort. A lot has been learned from these experiences, and it would be unfortunate if we attacked areas of regulation piece by piece, as they are falling apart, while allowing regulation to grow continually. When we are structuring reform in one area, we can build on what we have learned from other areas—what kinds of administrative rules work well and what kinds do not work well.

At the same time, the multifaceted framework, as is found in the administration's energy bill, is promising. Taxes, rules, standards, and antitrust are all found in the same parts of the bill. Based upon what we have learned from experience, we have to structure the framework for the particular reform area. I think that energy and environment present opportunities for this approach, both because they are important and because, in dealing with them, we can learn so much from the other areas of regulation that are currently targets of opportunity. In the process of reform, we can try to institutionalize some of our experience.

PROFESSOR PELTZMAN: I hesitate to use the word *adverse* because it is a loaded term. In terms of the largest economic effects, however, the types of regulation that cut across many industries—for example, in the areas of energy and the environment—merit first consideration.

We sometimes talk as if we know what these regulations are supposed to do. We know that environmental regulation is supposed to remove environmental externalities, and we have at least some conception of what energy regulation is aimed at. But do we know how well regulation is doing its job? I do not think we do.

PROFESSOR NOLL: The question about the biggest mistakes can be formulated in two different ways. One is to frame the question as Professor MacAvoy has—namely, what specific industries or regulatory problems generate the largest costs to the economy? But I would like to suggest a second formulation—namely, what conceptual approaches to some real or imagined market problem have the least amount of common sense behind them? I would suggest four principles or ideas. Number one is the notion that price regulation is the way to deal with economic rents. Number two is that it makes sense to regulate inputs and product design, rather than outcomes, in the fields of health, safety, or the environment. Number three is that the appropriate way to think about priorities in the areas of health, safety, and environmental regulation is to reduce "hazard exposure." Number four is the notion that what affects the welfare of the management of a firm necessarily affects the welfare of consumers.

The first two ideas are obvious, but the last two can be considered in more detail. Reducing hazard exposure means that something is identified as dangerous and then those who are exposed to it are counted and are removed from exposure if they are sufficiently numerous. This is nonsensical for two reasons. First, it causes one to overlook the leverage one has in dealing with the problem. Some things are intrinsically hazardous and nothing can really be done about them except to ban them; they are not banned, however, because that would probably cause more loss of welfare than if they were allowed to continue. Thus, the "all or nothing" approach comes to "nothing," and the leverage of a program aimed at "something" is lost. Second, it causes one to overlook the fact that someone besides the person setting the regulation has some intelligence. Those substances that are the most hazardous and to which we are the most likely to be exposed are also those toward which we, as laborers or as consumers, are likely to develop our own strategy for avoidance. It is in the face of exposure to such substances highest on the "ban" list that the market is most likely to have worked already.

The idea that "what's good for General Motors is good for America" has played a role not only in regulation but also in tax policy such as in the example of the subsidy to the Lockheed Aircraft Corporation. The reasoning is that, if something happens so that a firm is threatened with bankruptcy or takeover, somehow that threatens its employees and its customers, and has a whole host of nasty economic consequences. The same logic is used in the case of broadcasting. The fact that television stations have capitalized values of licenses of $10 million to $20 million and that they would possibly go bankrupt if faced with competition is translated to mean that viewers would not get to watch television anymore, or that program sponsors would not get to advertise anymore. This line of reasoning identifies the survival of a particular firm with the continuation of service, but in most cases service will be provided by the firm taking over the remains, or by new entrants into the market. Thus, it is incorrect and misleading in regulatory policy to center on the regulated enterprise.

These are my candidates for the four most nonsensical ideas in regulatory policy. What is basically incorrect should be a prime target for a concerted reform movement.

5
What Changes Should Be Made in the Reform Process?

PROFESSOR MACAVOY: What changes can be made in the reform process to achieve results more quickly and at a lower cost to all concerned?

Several new tools to achieve reform have been proposed at various times. They include:

- "sunset" legislation, which would require periodic review of all government programs

- comprehensive reform legislation, which would reorganize or deregulate in sequence all transportation, energy, financial, and other agencies (including those in health and safety)

- legislative veto over commission decisions

- internal reform in the commissions, which would change the performance of the agency by new procedures or new personnel

- adoption of the old Ash Commission proposal, which called for most of the agencies to be moved into the Executive Office and to have their functions split between planning and adjudication.

The question is: Can the process of regulatory reform be improved by any of these devices?

MR. CUTLER: From my perspective as a lawyer who has struggled with the regulatory process, what is lacking most is the recognition that we need to balance many worthwhile goals against one another; even a country as rich and as multifarious as the United States has to make some choices. We do not really recognize that yet. In regulation, each agency is charged by the Congress with achieving a single mission or with looking out for one particular facet of a complex world. Even when environmental impact statements and inflation impact statements are required, they are prepared by the single-mission agency. So far as I know, there has never been an inflation impact statement prepared by an agency considering a regulation that did not find that the benefits of the proposed regulation outweighed the costs. The same thing is probably true about environmental impact statements. Experts located in single-mission agencies cannot achieve balance, and they should not be given that balancing function.

There is now no way to choose between an environmental goal and an energy conservation goal, or between a safety goal and an anti-inflation goal, except on a political basis. And those are extremely difficult political judgments that must be made after all possible expert advice has been gathered. By the same token, there is no way that the Congress can make each of those judgments on a regulation-by-regulation basis. That is why the Congress delegated the power to regulate to the agencies in the first place. Even though it is given a single mission, the standard the agency is always given is that it should do what is in the public interest.

Therefore, the only place to exercise this balancing function and to make someone accountable to the public for how it is exercised is to vest power in the President. At least the power to make the final decision on rule making should rest with the President in those cases in which he finds that what an agency proposed to do, or was failing to do, has a critical impact on achieving other major national goals.

Whether the President already has that power is a much debated and little understood proposition. I suppose that we all accept that the President cannot interfere in the process of the independent agencies—the classic group that includes the ICC, the FCC, and the CAB—but we seem to have carried over that notion to mean that he must not interfere even in the actions of the important regulatory agencies—like OSHA, NHTSA, and EPA—that are directly within the executive branch.

Moreover, there are many laws in which the regulatory power is conferred by statute, not to the President, but to the EPA administrator, the secretary of agriculture, the secretary of health, education, and welfare, and so on. We do not know what the President can do about regulatory reform, and we have no way of holding him accountable. We have no way of holding the Congress accountable. The best proof of this is that in the 1976 election both Jimmy Carter and Gerald Ford, as well as everybody in Congress or running for Congress, spoke out against the great problem of regulation and bureaucracy; they all demanded that something be done to reduce this terrible burden. None of them thought for a moment that he was talking about himself, or that he had in any way contributed to the problem. It was those "other fellows" out there.

This country badly needs to recognize that there must be a balancing function. The details of how to establish that function involve many political issues and concepts, ranging from questions about the proper roles of the Congress and the President to concerns about the dangers of an imperial presidency. Those details can be worked out, but the basic principle—that we must recognize the need for a balancing function and the need to assign that function to one individual or group—is a major priority.

PROFESSOR ROBINSON: I am very sympathetic to Lloyd Cutler's position, but it is important to lay on the table the implications of a presidential veto of the kind he has proposed. For the most part, we are talking not about the President but about the institutional White House, including the Council of Economic Advisers and anonymous staff below the level of the council. The President is not going to veto an FDA regulation on a new drug because such a regulation will probably never reach his attention.

Apart from the issue of whether the President should be given the power to veto proposed new agency regulations, the question arises about why he does not do more about regulatory reform than he does now. Certainly, the President has in his own person and through the institution of the White House an enormous influence. For the most part, however, very little of that influence has been used to change the regulatory process. I am reminded of a conference of regulators that President Ford took part in while he was in office. On the whole, the conference seemed to me to be a useful vehicle toward reform, in spite of the fact that the regulators delivered bunches of rhetorical flourishes saying, "We will be good," and then went home to do what they had always done before. Sustained attention on the part of the President, however, certainly cannot go unnoticed, even by an independent regulator. Thus, I think that the President and the White House have an enormous power to give direction to regulatory policy without any new laws being passed.

PROFESSOR PECK: During the Johnson administration, I chaired a group of deputy secretaries dealing with price and wage stability. The group was in terrible trouble from the moment it was created. It was launched with the President saying that this was a matter of such urgency that he would give it his personal attention. He appointed a committee of cabinet members who all said that this was a matter of such urgency that they would give it their personal attention. They, in turn, each appointed an assistant secretary and I never saw a cabinet member, let alone the President, associated with that group. So, it is true that these issues do go to the institutional White House, but they are decided at the staff level, unless they are so dramatic that they reach the President's attention—as occurred, for example, in President Kennedy's confrontation with the steel industry.

My experience has been, moreover, that most of the regulatory issues that we have been talking about attract the attention of the President only if they raise concerns about inflation. The problem is that, taken individually, the various regulatory measures add such a small amount to overall inflation that a President is reluctant to spend his political capital on them. The cumulative impact, however, may or may not be quite substantial; we really do not know about that. On the whole, however, the referral system has not worked well to date.

Despite these cautions, I think that in our system of government the people around the President are probably the ones who can best look at the general public interest—indeed, they may be the only ones who can do so. The particular agencies necessarily have to be concerned with the health of their industries and not so much with the cost of controls to society. Thus, I see certain merits and limitations to having the President or the institutional White House be the chief regulator.

PROFESSOR MACAVOY: I would like to turn to the internal reform process in the commissions. Professor Breyer, does it make a difference if the institutional White House turns its searchlight on the commissions and agencies and says, "We are going to propose and appoint better commissioners"?

PROFESSOR BREYER: In the case of the CAB, the answer is yes. We have seen the results.

DR. SNOW: Internal reform can do some good, but it can also do some mischief, because the notion that good men will reform commissions gets in the way of the kind of fundamental institutional change that is needed—namely, to remove regulation, or at least reduce regulation significantly, and let the marketplace work.

I think that there is a real risk in this notion that we can appoint good men and they will solve the problem. Good men can make enormous changes, but their terms come to an end and they may be followed by people who are not so capable or so motivated. The real attention and energy should be directed toward fundamental reform so that the agency's regulatory function is fitted more appropriately to the underlying economic realities.

PROFESSOR BREYER: I have never heard a President say, "I am going to do an amazing thing. I am going to appoint bad people." Even those who recommend individuals to the President do not say, "I want you to appoint my friend X; he is a bad person." They say, "He is a good person."

MR. ROBSON: Internal reform can do something to solve the problems connected with economic regulation. In the long run, however, institutional change and a fundamental change in direction are required, and that demands congressional action. Otherwise, reform is left to the vagaries of the appointment process. As Professor Breyer pointed out, no one intentionally appoints a "bad" person to an agency, but sometimes the views of the appointees differ markedly from the views of those who have preceded or may follow them.

In keeping with Lloyd Cutler's concept of political accountability, fundamental changes in the regulatory process should be national decisions, not the decisions of three out of five people who happen to be sitting on an agency at a particular time. Moreover, if I were looking at this issue of regulatory reform from the outside, I would insist that the redirection be reliable and durable, and I think that those characteristics can be achieved only by an act of Congress.

PROFESSOR NOLL: Legislative change is the only mechanism for long-term change in regulatory processes, outcomes, and breadth of mandate. Thus, what I am about to say should not be misconstrued—I have not suddenly become a convert to the Ash Commission report, or anything like that. But I do not think that the choice has to be restricted to either internal reform or legislative change; there is an alternative.

Contrary to many of the comments that have been made during this discussion, in the past few years members of Congress have grown substantially smarter about the problems of implementing regulation and about the failures of regulation. Some of them even have come to believe academic arguments about better ways to define both the boundaries of regulation and the instruments used to effect change within those boundaries in order to reduce regulatory inefficiencies. Nevertheless, the congressmen are still uncertain and unsure. They do not really trust economists because we do not have a stake in the results, except insofar as the predictive accuracy of our work affects our standing before the promotion and review committees in academic life. Among congressmen, many of those who voted against deregulation of natural gas and who were initially reluctant to bring the airline regulatory reform bill to a final vote basically believe the research results but are afraid.

In this context, the notion of internal reform becomes an important way station in an uncertain journey to deregulation or substantive legislative regulatory reform. The same subcommittee of the Congress that just a few short years ago was very upset with critical hearings on the airline industry is today perfectly happy with the present "reformist" management of the CAB. The members of that subcommittee allowed the commission to engage in a "deregulation experiment" and eventually said: "Okay, the experiment started by John Robson and continued by Alfred Kahn and Betsy Bailey worked. The world did not come to an end. Grand Rapids still has airline service. Let's go ahead and substantially reduce the intervention of the CAB into the industry."

What does this imply about the role of the executive office in reform? First, the legislative approach to reform alone probably will not work. The grand mistake of the Ford administration's approach to regulatory reform was pinning reform entirely on legislation, going to the Congress with all those reform bills. They should have been just as active in making certain that reformists were appointed to the commissions. Such appointments are not an effective long-term solution, but they provide the Congress with the chance to experiment with reform while they still retain control of the process, or while they are still able, through oversight activities and through banging on the agencies, to bring back "the good old days" if the experiment goes wrong.

It may well be that even reform in the trucking industry is not totally dead. Internal reform of the ICC may be a way station to getting a truck deregulation bill through the Congress five to ten years from now. But the reform of the ICC certainly cannot be accomplished in the same way as that of the CAB; it will not be enough to pick the right person to be chairman of that eleven-headed monster. The ICC is just too cumbersome an agency. Thus, the first step would be a structural reorganization of the ICC that reduces the number of commissioners to five or seven and changes various other purely structural aspects of the process. The second step would be to say, "Now let us experiment with having some pro-competitive people run the ICC. We will appoint a new chairman who, in turn, can put together a staff and conduct a three- or four-year experiment in reducing the scope and content of controls. In the end, if it all works out, there will be legislation."

This "way station" approach will work well as long as the right boundaries and mix of policy instruments have been established for regulation. And the premise of Lloyd Cutler's argument is that regulation already is pretty sensible, both in terms of its purposes and in terms of its instruments. Before that statement can be made, however, a whole lot of reforming has to be done and, in that process, I do not think that the White House's veto and oversight mechanism is going to help solve current problems. But if all these reformist commissioners are appointed and if all these reform bills are eventually passed, then that White House mechanism might have an effect.

MR. CUTLER: The bulk of present regulation is not okay. I do not think that it is by a long shot. But most of the things that are being regulated probably have to be regulated. At least, the political consensus that they have to be is going to last for a long time.

The fault with regulation is not as much the fault of the statute as it is of the impasse that exists within each agency. One procompetitive chairman is fine, but why has no President ever appointed a working reformist majority? There are very few things in the CAB reform bill that a working majority of the CAB could not have accomplished all by itself. The procedures could have been speeded up, and the carriers could have been allowed to put rate-cutting devices of one kind or another into operation. The only reasons that these and other reforms have not been carried out are the political pressures within each agency preventing any such changes and the lack of interest and will on the part of most Presidents to change the situation.

In the case of some of the directly regulated industries—such as the CAB-regulated airline industry—I agree that the tide is changing, and there is the chance that they will receive the healthy dose of deregulation they need. What worries me far more, though, are the cut-across regulations—the OSHA regulations, emissions standard regulations, water quality regulations, regulations about pension funds mandated by the Employee Retirement Income Security Act (ERISA) of 1974, and so on. Those are the real problems, and I do not see the slightest sign that the Congress is disillusioned with that kind of regulation. Nothing is cut out, and more is added every year.

Unsettled Questions on Regulatory Reform, edited by Paul W. MacAvoy, presents a broad range of views by authorities on government, law, and economics, on the following questions:

- Why has so little regulatory reform been accomplished?
- Has the case for deregulation been made?
- What are the priority areas for reform?
- Where is regulation having the greatest effect?
- What changes should be made in the reform process?

The participants in this discussion are:

JOHN W. BARNUM
Former deputy secretary of transportation

STEPHEN G. BREYER
Harvard University

LLOYD N. CUTLER
Wilmer, Cutler & Pickering

HENDRIK S. HOUTHAKKER
Harvard University

PAUL JOSKOW
Massachusetts Institute of Technology

PAUL W. MACAVOY (moderator)
Yale University

ROGER G. NOLL
Former director, Government Regulation Studies, Brookings Institution

MERTON J. PECK
Yale University

SAM PELTZMAN
University of Chicago

GLEN O. ROBINSON
Former commissioner, Federal Communications Commission

JOHN E. ROBSON
Former chairman, Civil Aeronautics Board

ANTONIN SCALIA
University of Chicago

JOHN W. SNOW
Former administrator, National Highway Traffic Safety Administration

RICHARD E. WILEY
Former chairman, Federal Communications Commission

$2.75

 American Enterprise Institute for Public Policy Research
1150 Seventeenth Street, N.W., Washington, D.C. 20036